WIND LEAVES ABSENCE

WIND LEAVES ABSENCE

MARY MAXWELL

thistledown press

Thistledown Press Ltd.
410 2nd Avenue North
Saskatoon, Saskatchewan, S7K 2C3
www.thistledownpress.com

Library and Archives Canada Cataloguing in Publication
Maxwell, Mary, author
Wind leaves absence / Mary Maxwell.

Poems.
ISBN 978-1-77187-100-6 (paperback)
I. Title.
PS8626.A8855W55 2016   C811'.6   C2016-901047-3

Cover artwork by Philip J. Curtis courtesy of Philip C Curtis Charitable Trust for the Encouragement of Art, Philip J. Curtis and Jane Ellis, Co-Trustees
Cover and book design by Jackie Forrie
Printed and bound in Canada

Canada Council   Conseil des Arts
for the Arts   du Canada

SASKATCHEWAN
ARTS BOARD

Canada

Thistledown Press gratefully acknowledges the financial assistance of the Canada Council for the Arts, the Saskatchewan Arts Board, and the Government of Canada through the Canada Book Fund for its publishing program.

Acknowledgements

Grateful acknowledgement is made to the following publications in whose pages these poems first appeared: *Grain Magazine, NeWest Review, Descant, Listening with the Ear of the Heart, CV2*.

Permission was granted to use quotations from Elizabeth Brewster's *Jacob's Dreams* (Oberon, 2002), Michael Crummey's "Her Mark" in *Hard Light: Brick Books Classics 5* (Brick Books, 2015), John Livingston Clark's *Body and Soul* (Exile Editions, 2002), Catherine Gildiner's *Coming Ashore* (ECW, 2014), Edna St. Vincent Millay's, "Dirge without Music", *The Buck in the Snow and other poems*, 1928, courtesy of the Millay Society, Anne Michaels' *Fugitive Pieces* (McClelland & Stewart, a division of Penguin Random House Canada Limited, 1996) and Gregory David Roberts', *Shantaram: A Novel*, (St Martin's Press, 2004).

Thanks to the Saskatchewan Artists/Writers Retreats program, St Peter's Abbey, and to Thistledown Press for the publication of this book.

Thanks to Honor Kever and Daphne Kotzer for their encouragement, support, and wisdom. Dave Margoshes for his insight, skill, and generosity of spirit. Sylvia Legris for her enthusiastic support of my work. Annette Bower for her humor. Shelley Banks for the author photograph.

The writers-in-residence at the Saskatoon Public Library: Betsy Warland, John L. Clarke, Dave Margoshes, Jeanette Lynes, Anne Simpson, and John Donlan. Tim Lilburn, Myrna Kostash, Laura Burkhart, Edna Alford, and Geoffrey Ursell for help along the way. Linda Fisher and Dr Heather Brenneman for their skill in assisting me to regain my health and pursue the completion of the manuscript.

To Josh Pendleton and Kate Pendleton for your love and support. You get it.

Always and with great affection and appreciation to William (Bill) Robertson for your great and abiding love and encouragement, patience and kindness during the writing of this manuscript. Your skill and generosity fortified and grounded me during the many revisions of this work.

CONTENTS

OTHERS

In memory of all those who have gone before.

Memory is not reality. It does not give an accurate picture of the past . . . every memory gets shifted through our unconscious needs . . . family members do not share memories, they share events. They have all taken shards of the past and put them together into either a slightly skewed or drastically different picture. They see and interpret them through their own lens of need . . . We all believe our own realities.

— Catherine Gildiner, Coming Ashore

Bystander

Like a bystander
grief waits.

Takes its place at the table
an empty chair in the corner.

Hangs in the wilderness between words
sighs   whispers.

It appears at family gatherings
filling in margins, around things unsaid

prayers unanswered.

Grief arrives when we meet for tea

the telling of lies.

An empty gust
            through the open door.

FATHER

Empty closet

My father rummages in his closet
searching for lost papers
a favourite sweater

Trousers fall from hangers
collapse on the floor

He pulls out a tweed jacket, discards
suits that have grown too large

he roots through drawers, dumps the penny jar

His diminishing frame
shadows the doorway

Empty hangers
jangle

Adrift

A book in his hand
he turns the pages
tells me the words
don't make sense.

A novel, one he's read
but can't get past the first paragraph.

They tell me I have dementia
enunciating each syllable   trying

to decipher its meaning
how to understand the loss.

The darkening room.

The fumbling with pages.

A jumble of words.

Set adrift.

Enigma

His brain an organic puzzle
he works to break the code
pry language out of the taps
and dashes of memory, a maze
with crooked passages
dead ends.

He forgets how to place
one foot in front
of the other
the stairs
the ups and downs
the place he calls home
the daily maze of the kitchen.

My father says *there are holes in my history*
apologizes for slowing me down
pushing his walker through wet matted leaves.

Yes, father you are
slowing me down
so I can walk with you
a few more hours
offer you my arm
my inadequate words
in the softly falling rain.

Late autumn, a garden

We sit on a bench in the withered garden
my father tells me *there are blanks*
where words and names used to be.
He taps his cane on the dying grass
his winter face bewildered
when I ask about his life
eager for a final story.

It's too late, he says
So much has gone
I wonder where?

Leaving my father's house

Stacks in every room: newspapers, books, magazines
radios in three rooms playing election results
charts and scribblings, notes
on everything.

Prayer books, bibles, maps of genealogy
he's trying to find his way into history, locate his people
find his way home.

Scribbling into margins of his prayer books
the Oblate breviary, Good News Bible
he wrestles with God, pleading help with patience
Help me Lord, he writes, *help me, a sinner.*

The hermit monk who considered him brother
told me once: "your dad tends towards scrupulosity"
I see it now in these scribblings, this bargaining.

He asks forgiveness daily
on every page, prayers begging
a reluctant God
beseeches help to pray better
not harden his heart or be unkind.

Today I open the door to his house
see him silent in another room
studying, seeking a way home
to God.

House by the Sea

If the brain is a house by the sea
dementia a storm rising
water rushes in, lifts tables, chairs
family, friends
      all float away.

Mute, deaf and blind, the brain
employs the body as translator
muteness into spoken word
deafness into birdsong
blindness into a vision of heaven.

Despite this violent plunder
within my father's diminished brain
dwells gratitude — that rare and final virtue
that defines him.
Thank you for bringing me here — to this — this place.

This place is the sea, we sit
listening to waves, the snap
of kites flying high.

Birds swoop and soar
their frantic cries lost
in the wind, the waves.
Boats lean on silver water.

The brain may not be a house by the sea
but a house, anywhere
its windows
wide open.

Tangles

After the storm I walk home in dying light
balance on January ruts, one step, another
stoop under pine branches, tangles of icy shards
on green needles, tingling bits of broken glass.

At work I learn about the tangle diseases
ALS, Parkinson's, Lewy Body dementia, Alzheimer's —
the peculiar pattern of neurofibrillary tangles
the slow theft of words, mobility, balance.

My father's brain a snarled web
confused fibers that stole recognition
of the familiar: can opener, spatula, wooden spoon
Agnosia.

Wit and wisdom sealed off
as useless plaques formed
his marvellous brain now confused
by the markings on a page
a pen, once an extension of his hand.

Slivers of ice
break off
fall on frozen ground.

His people

My father holds the photo album
peers at the black and white images
sets it down
looks out the window
the rain-blurred garden.

He picks it up again
rubs the coarse pages, touches the faces
turns the page.

I tell him that toddler in the picture is him
in his grandmother's arms, her Ottawa garden, 1923
taken there to see his mother's people
part of the lie that included baptizing him
far from the Protestant town where he was born
held by a priest from the Ottawa valley

the water warm on his prairie brow.

Line on paper

You had a horse, didn't you Dad?
Yes, Sandy. He saved my life.

I hand him a piece of paper, a pencil
he holds it in his left hand
as if it's another finger
as if it's always been there
holds it with such intention and purpose
pulls the lead in one diagonal line.

From all the times he's drawn this line
I know it's Sandy's neck.

He puts the pencil down, looks at me,
doesn't know
what the next line should be.

Hammer

1

The boy hears his mother's cries
giving birth on a fall day.

His sister placed in the wooden box
her hand cold as a doll's.

Hears the sound of his father hammering
the box on the back step, lid nailed shut.

2

Sleigh bells on Christmas Eve
the doctor's cutter rushing into the yard.

Birth of his brother
his mother crying.

The doctor leaving, shaking his head as he pulls
his fur hat down over his ears.

Standing at the window, the boy wipes away
frost, watches the horse's breath, ice crystals in the air

wonders about baby Jesus
Santa, the reindeer.

His father pulls on his boots
goes out into the dark.

The boy hears the sound of hammering
in the shop behind the barn.

3

Fifty years later his own sons die
and he's never learned
to use a hammer.

In her arms

After TB Grandma came west to a dry climate
taught embroidery, silver needles
piercing white muslin.

Married, moved to a farm, a granary house
filled with dust. An abiding need for penance.

Offered up life's trials: hostile soil, three stillborn children,
a husband silenced by their drought of love, a man confused
by her devotion to a church that claimed
their children would never see God.

Found solace in St Theresa, needlework
summer flowers on the windowsill.

In holy pictures St Theresa cradles a sheaf of roses
promising to let fall a shower of petals
miracles and other favours for those devoted
to her little way. In need of miracles Grandma
pleaded for a rain of daily grace.

In her garden Grandmother walks among blue
delphiniums, pinks and lavender, yellow sunflowers
wild against the shelterbelt.

She fed and watered, morning and evening
trimmed and pruned
cradled the cut stalks
in her arms like children.

Orphan

Aunt Lily asks for *no flowers* at Grandfather's funeral
only dried wheat stalks please
Bearded Durum/ No. 1 Hard/ Marquis
tied with rust coloured ribbon
tearing in the wind.

My father lays flowers on his mother's grave
three infants beside her
marked with single concrete discs
the cold prairie soil.

An orphan now, my father
releases a handful of clay
Requiem pace.

Moving on

My father has left his house
moved down a corridor
of darkness
a mumble of wheelchairs
jumble of smells
strangers
behind closed doors

windows that don't open.

Good news

I watch from the doorway as his bright eyes
dart around the hospital room
Edgar across, Leo beside him
a new man in the bed by the window.
My father watches, laughs along with them
but has no words.

We wheel him into the spring air
he sees the newspaper box, turns sharply
in his chair, scrutinizing headlines.

We deposit coins, hand him the damp paper
he holds it close, smells the ink, looks
at the headlines, the old newspaper man
grips it tightly on his lap.

Unable to make sense of the day's drama
politics, firestorms, obituary columns —
he hangs onto that paper
for dear life.

Two step

In hospital my father
sits in the hallway
waiting.

He watches as a stranger
walks by. Waits for
the kindness of the hour:
a smile, a gesture.

Nurses lift him up
walk on either side of him, joking
they're doing the two-step

> At the family reunion
> I dance with my father round and
> round, two-step in the Plenty hall.

He laughs as they swing him
into bed, settle him for sleep.

Still a little dance
in the old dancer, still.

Away

On visits my father kisses my hands
pulls me into an awkward hug
How did you ever find me?

Lost among strangers
peculiar faces, acrid odors
a hallway of mirrors.

He shuffles his feet, moves his wheelchair
into his own dance
that slowly
inexorably

reels him away.

Rosary

I lift the pale rose from its vase
petals fall to the floor
I kneel and find his rosary
fallen under his hospital bed.

Ten years old on my knees reciting the rosary
my father leading the way
eight of us murmuring response.

Five decades: fifty Hail Marys, five Glory-bes
two Our Fathers, a total of fifty-seven prayers
every night, thirty-one days
one thousand seven hundred sixty-seven prayers.

Windows wide, robin's evening song
clear and sweet. Catholics inside praying
Protestants outside shouting spring.

Tonight, forty years on, a thousand miles from home
I hand my father his rosary, he twines the beads around my hands
lifting each strand over and under my fingers, saying
this is what my mother used to do.

Language nearly gone, his prayers
still here. Catholics are sweet
inside with rosaries.
Protestants whistle, mopping
up the hall.

Birthday

When we asked our father to sign
mother's 75th birthday card, he paused
said, *I don't remember*
how to spell
wonderful.

Few words

My father speaks only a few words now:
hymns, prayers, recitations of the rosary.

A prophet in our home, his authority reining us in
at the dinner table, thundering about incomplete doctrines
epistolary truths, political diatribes
challenging us to question him
engage in argument.

He's lost that thunder now
just a word spoken thoughtfully
after a long look into my eyes or a sigh
while he gazes at the rain-blurred window
the sheared green hedge, rhododendron blossoms
fallen to the ground.

I am one of three daughters who visit
spooning puréed food and encouragement
into his silence, eyes following as I reach
for the custard in child-sized dishes.

We join other daughters who wheel the old
tyrants down cluttered hallways.

Fathers gone soft as pudding
unable to take us hostage anymore.

Choking

In the nursing home, the aide says my father is choking
on his food.

"Stroke his throat," she tells us, "remind him to swallow
his thickened fluids, puréed food."

He holds soup in his mouth
it dribbles down his chin.
I spoon it away.

After church we visit again. He begins to cough
eyes pleading. He cannot speak.

The staff tell us he choked
on a sandwich at lunch.
A sandwich?
They suctioned, couldn't get the food out.

He sits in his wheelchair, breathing in short
wheezing gasps, a paroxysm of coughing
his face turns purple.

I touch his shoulders, speak quietly.
It doesn't help.

Old man's friend

I say

Send him to hospital.

It's the weekend.

One doctor on call.

Doctor arrives.

Calls the ambulance.

Paramedics give him oxygen.

Take him to hospital.

I ride with him.

Try to calm him.

In emergency they anaesthetize him.

Doctor explains.

Larynx is bruised.

Blood vessels broken.

Choked on food.

Aspirated into his lungs.

"He'll have pneumonia now."

The doctor closes the chart.

"We call it the old man's friend."

Last time

The last time I saw my father
he was waiting for the bath
slumped in his wheelchair
head forward, eyes closed.

I kissed his cool brow, whispered
I love you
told him I was leaving the next day
might see him again soon.

(The lies we tell when death is near)

I meant to return but
the weight of a final good-bye
my legs too heavy to walk back.

I told myself he'd be sleeping —
wrapped in the warm flannel night.

Brief dance

For Elizabeth Brewster

A west coast spring, daffodil
blossoms drooping, prayer-like.
Soft rain hums the air, the cool green song
hardly a lament.

I tell my friend about my longing to live
by the sea among fragrant flowers
perpetual spring — home by my father's side
as his words disappear and his light fades.
I tell her of my father's bewilderment
with loss: memory, faith, family.

She reads me two benedictions from
The Amidah, Blessing in Spring:
how thin a surface
supports our lives,
makes possible our brief dance
through the seasons

When I return home to winter in Saskatchewan
I remember her words:
It's difficult to bless winter
the bleak white streets
under the cold glare of the sun

But, as always, winter
falters into spring
trees bend in the rain
blossoms fall.

My father dies on a long green evening.

I bow my head and whisper
the 23rd Psalm
stumble into spring.

He closed his eyes

We flower . . . the wind blows . . . we are gone.

— Psalm 103

My sister says it was the sound
of rags tearing, his breath an infrequent gasp.

His body heaved, tried to breathe
one clean line.

A kiss from all
children, grandchildren, wife
who left yesterday, gone for the summer
to a lake a thousand miles away.

He closed his eyes.

Tears. My sister's.
My brother's bowed head.

Spiritus, breath

Open the windows
set the spirit free.

When my father died

I wanted to be there to witness his last
ragged breaths, his spirit restless for release
hold his hand as his body lost its warmth
his heart slowed.

I could have read the psalms, recited his favourite prayers
sung *Shall We Gather at the River.*

Confessed I was first in the family to push limits
punished, grounded every weekend
shamed in front of the others.

Confessed I hated him when I was fifteen
how he chose my sister as princess in our childhood plays
my brother the prince
me, the wicked witch.

Confessed I was the one to name demons, expose lies
of everlasting life in exchange for his long service.
The church that denied how alcohol crept in through closed doors
killing us one at a time, with little redemption:
uncles, cousins, brothers, an aunt who died in the mental home.

The noonday demon threatened to devour him
me at thirty, our mother, silenced by too many children
a church that kept us poor
in body, mind, and spirit.

A church that went back on promises of salvation
whiskey priests who forbade us to be angry.

I wanted to be there so he could have spoken my name
as if I were the only child.
But I did not get there in time.

I could have told him I loved him.

My father's funeral

His ashes on the altar
a photograph, gaudy bouquets.

An incense burner swinging, its sooty smoke
screens a play I don't want to see.

Hovering priests chanting
the mass for the dead.

We stand in a row, a strange church
burial rites, a familiar ritual.

Psalms, prayers we know by heart
lips too numb to form the words
hymns stuck in our throats.

The church hall filled with friends
relatives, ex-husbands, wives.

We stand in a row shaking hands
are pulled into the arms
of strangers.

Later at the graveside
the family plot, opened.

Our faces ruined by the loss
our centre gone, it cannot hold.

Memory, a door hanging
one hinge holding.

The last of the funeral

Orchids
in the slender vase
by the window

Petal skin choked
fallen over
gone dry

In another room
my birthday flowers
loudly proclaim spring

Photograph

A silver frame holds my father now
luminescent hands folded in the foreground.

The charcoal vest from Santorini
too large on his diminishing frame
its closed loops hanging.
Silver hands, silver hair, his smile
almost transparent.

In the photograph I see
his eyes alive with memories:
bouzouki music playing Zorba
his arms lifted, my mother
dancing.

I hear his voice
and I know it:

daughter, dear daughter.

BROTHERS

Needle

Listening to Doug's story I remember
that time in the hospital visiting
a sick friend, sitting on his bed
getting loaded, straight scotch
from his medicine cup, curtains pulled
around us, eighteen and beyond reproach.

Who did I think I was when each day
blurred into the next?
Wearing my starched white uniform
to a Hallowe'en party. It was all a masquerade
the memorized script, patient care plans
nuns swishing down the corridors.

I remember the guy with the DTs
flailing arms tied to the bedrails
room kept darkened to diminish delusions
legs bleeding from scratching the bugs off
the tremors, bed banging against
a concrete wall, teeth clattering, moaning
until I drove in the needle, scraping
against his scrawny hipbone.

My brother Tom spoke briefly of his life
his walks into Clinton Creek
from his squatter's cabin, reading Robert Service
caught by the spell of the Yukon
sometimes on those visits to town he'd lose
two days, wake up, not know where he was
or who.

He came back from Bogota skinny
wired, aiming his gun from his truck window
believed he was robbed, his tools missing.
Friends asked what to do?
Put him in hospital, I said.

Did they tie him down, keep the room
dark so the demons would not
devour him?
Did some young nurse stand bewildered
beside this wild young man, her needle
poised to deliver him?

Fool

I'm standing in line at The Bay to buy
a pair of pants for my brother's corpse
naked and swollen from
botched embalming.

The funeral home slits the pants to make them fit.
His body a stranger's — distorted from the crash.
They pinch and pull his face
makeup caked at the corners of his eyes
across the abrasion on his cool brow

prepared to look right
for the viewing.

Like Lear's fool
I despair
surrender to noonday demons
go to bed
leave the script.

One Hundred Pink Roses

Elegant and curled
Is the blossom. Fragrant is the blossom . . .
More precious was the light in your eyes than all the roses in the world.
— Edna St Vincent Millay, "Dirge Without Music"

The day of his funeral
a bouquet of roses arrives at my door
my fingers blunt as wooden blocks
I untie the ribbon, it falls to the floor.

Thirty-seven signatures, men from the silver mine
the Dempster crew. Yukon men
loved my brother, their foreman —
what a great guy.

He lies still and cold in the coffin
tissue gas distorting
his neck, chin, mouth

while at home each rose lifts to the light.

After the funeral brothers and sisters go east and west
parents go home
all of us leaving

the room empty

Rose petals curl, begin to fade
fall to the floor, a small sound
a sigh   a whisper
on the bare hardwood.

I can't decide what to do with them.

Alone in the Cathedral

Where is the way to the dwelling of the light
And where is the place of darkness,
That you may take it to its territory
And that you may discern the paths to its home?

— Job 38

I walked out of your funeral
out of the magnificent cathedral
a line of mighty priests chanting —
the mass of the dead.

I went home, wrote you letters
tried yoga, counselling, dream work, philosophy classes
meditation, medication, other churches, the Unitarians
for God's sake.

Followed the path of darkness
walked the recesses of the deep
tried to find the dwelling of the light
my way home again.

A Wise Heart

What caused you to forget
that your legacy was plain Saskatchewan
soil both your grandfathers knew?

What sentenced you to wander the Yukon
live in a cabin at Clinton Creek
die in the shadow of Tombstone mountains?

Today I wander among men I call brothers
break bread and sing.
The cantor's sweet tenor leads vespers
across the chapel, into the hallway and out
over the fields, the garden and orchard, heavy with fruit.

His monk's face could be yours my lost brother
deep set eyes, hands riven with motor oil
about your age, had you lived.

You could have found refuge here, too
among farmers and sons of farmers, men
who lift their voices in praise, four times daily.

Monks and brothers singing across the chapel
weeding in the garden, tending the bees
pruning the orchard, souls
for the final harvest.

Living among the breakage

Eliot knew it. So did Conan Doyle.
Dogs barking in the night.
The hounds of midnight tearing
a hole in the summer dark.
Their howls keep me awake.

Uncles dead from the drink, an aunt locked up
Great grandfather paying a gambling debt with a child's pony
Horsewhip across the back of mother's legs
Grandma's blue dress burned in the stove
Others snorting coke behind the furnace
dropping acid, toking hash
knocking back whiskey, chugging beer
punching a hole in the wall

car crashes, one, two, three, four, driving
off bridges, under water, under
ground.

We are lost and lonely
dogs howling in the night.

Fracture line

My son heaves his body into mountains
wrestles with trees in thick white cloaks
twists and turns against
the hard rock face.

Someday he'll learn to go
with the mountain, follow
the way it curves the light,
climb to Everest's base
cross avalanche fracture lines
and live to find the secret —
what it is
to be a man.

I had a brother once who smashed
headlong into traffic, drove off a bridge
into Yukon water, at 21
wore 50 stitches across his face —
punched his way through the Klondike
wrestled with Euclids on the Dempster
holed up in a cabin outside
Clinton Creek alone with a gun
a dog, Al Purdy's poetry
lame from a mangled leg
   lack of love
    booze and cocaine.

At 25 he lost his way outside Faro
that first Sunday in spring
still searching for the secret.

Yukon

The car stops. We stare
into the great alone.

We've come north to see
where he lived, worked, died.

The landscape's open heart
breaking beauty, its dancefloor
nearly empty.

Across the wide valley dall sheep
bow their curled heads, mountains
rise up. Bluebirds, varied thrush, warblers
an eagle soars. A migrant's symphony.

Tatshenshini mirage on the horizon
its silver vein through viridian green.
Five Finger Rapids swirling
deep with survivors' stories
the ones who didn't make it.

The river's curve is enough
to hold a man, ground him
in summer, a primal voice
to soothe his raucous soul
until winter takes hold
and kills everything.

Alone in his snowbound cabin, gold fever
in his words, his dreams
my brother walks into town once a month
across that permanent frozen heart
to let loose what stalked his wild youth.

On the back of a photo of the Yukon river:
I'm entirely possessed by the spell
I love it so much I'm never going to leave.

Search

We walk the boardwalks of Dawson City
my mother and I searching
for her lost son, my brother.
Thirty-two years since he's gone but
someone here might remember him.

A tall dark-haired man
darts around a corner ahead.
I quicken my steps, follow.
But he's gone
no sign he was ever there.
A ghost town.

Truth is a bully

Truth is a bully we all pretend to like.

— Gregory David Roberts, *Shantaram*

Truth gangs up, pummels you with facts
A phone call
"your brother Tom is dead"
    frozen ground
    thrown from the van
    no seatbelt
    Autopsy in black and white
    Yukon highway, mile 252
    flailed chest, broken clavicles, severed
    vessels, dead on impact

Truth blasts into dreams, plays in slow mo
    His voice shouting: Oh no

Two years later the police at my door
The radio announces each and every hour
    "Car crash on Warman road — two dead"
    his name: Christopher, my brother
    Police report: speed of the car, new blacktop
    drowns headlights

    El Camino gliding like an iron coffin
    hits a steel blockade, Berber–Green paving machine

    dead on impact

    the morgue
    his face inert on the slab
    the impossible angle of his arm

Truth stands in the pulpit preaching:
    Big. Happy. Catholic.

As children we confessed our little sins, act
of contrition
did our penance: sixhailmarysfourourfathers
fiveglorybes.

No salvation

Cursed: not holy.

Truth armors you with arrogance
bullies you with false beliefs
The truth the whole truth and nothing but the truth
So help me God.

Truth turns the pack against you
keeps you isolated and alone
days and nights its vertiginous path
winds its way inward
you lose all balance, all sense.

Truth is a bully we all pretend to like.

Of fairy tales and princes

In our story it wasn't the youngest
son who captured the golden goose.
When his turn came to seek his fortune
he didn't find the magic well
make his way through the labyrinth
slay the dragon or free the princess
and marry her.

He was invaded by an unknown enemy
forces that marched their troops through his body
occupied his organs, swelled his slim torso
moved into words until his language
spat curses across barrooms
family reunions.

This son travelled but did not prosper in abundance
did not acquire wisdom from failures of other brothers.
His voyage between police and the bottle, his smokes, the acid
friends who carried him
C'mon just for one night.

When he returned from the last night out
his vessel flew no victory flags
no fables round the campfire
his body limp
in the ruined car.

Priest

I saw great trouble in my brothers' eyes
wonder about that prince of the church
who prowled around our Ottawa house
in the early 70s
how he took my dark-eyed brothers
for rides in his sleek Thunderbird
away to his isolated cabin to swim
the long summer afternoons
my parents turning them over to him.
After all, a priest.

Forty years later I learn this prince
is sent to jail for abusing boys.
But not before the bishops hid him in Rome
bestowing a Vatican appointment
that absolved his sin.

dead drunk

blunt words
knock the piss guts breath

onto the night highway
ignite the white siren
again

dead drunk

not *impaired, inebriated*
those civilized words
expressing intemperance

death by drowning in toxins
leaving a pool
infinite sorrow

lipsmouththroat a vise
grief's blunt instrument
pries open
o no o god no

driving drunk on a northern road
is like walking into a lake
with your pockets full of stones.

Hot, cold

The last time I saw you drunk at my back door, you smiled
too widely, leaned against the green house
asked to take my children for ice-cream
such a hot day.

The last time I talked to you in prison
you said you'd given up drinking
you were doing better since
our brother's death, your girl's leaving.

You told me how you carried your struck-down dog
across the street, a dark blot in your arms
her head hanging bloody
staining your jeans.

The last time I touched you
cold and crooked in the morgue drawer
your face was like a child lost in sleep
a slight rictus grin
your plaid shirt torn open at the shoulder.

Police

I rode my Harley into the police station
up the stairs to the holding cells.
Told off the cops, signed the papers.
Hauled my brother, bloodied with a broken nose
the hell out of there, making promises
I couldn't keep.

The night after

I identify my brother's body in the morgue
I wander the house, unable to sleep
steal into rooms, sit on the floor beside my son —
listen to him breathing, his sweet breath
even and deep, his covers rising and falling.

Those days I held my infant brother,
nights when my always pregnant mother
was too tired to get up one more time,
I crooned songs about sunshine and birds,
nursery rhymes, whatever tune would soothe
the night terrors that visited him even then
held him until his breath was even and deep
his head heavy on my shoulder.

Shoulders

The day he died my daughter fell
down the stairs, hurt her foot
and could not walk.

Two days later we filed into the funeral
parlour, a family event.

My brother who used to carry her
is among us but cannot lift her
on his shoulders.

He lies cold in the coffin
his corpse made beautiful.

I lift her, set her on a bench
she looks at his sleeping face.

At five she knows only the uncle
who carried her on his shoulders
above everyone else.

She sees his familiar plaid shirt
wonders why he's so still, why
she's so much taller than him.

Wind Leaves Absence

Uilleann pipes skirl with the piper's breath
           eleven and tall in my ancestral tartan
           I dance over crossed swords
           lift my hands to the music,
           step into the arms of the dance

           Ten years later we gather at Christmas and dance
           in Hull, La Chaudiere tavern
           my brothers, one home from the north
           another who loved stories
           dance me in their arms
           round and round till I can
           hardly breathe

Within two years both brothers
dead.

No wake.

Funeral March, 1981

Three brothers, three sisters carry his body
thirteen stairs to the cathedral door
we leave my brother's body at the altar
four priests and a bishop who never knew him
stand high on the altar, incense, candles
tight lamentations.

Amazing grace
how sweet the sound
the pipe's low moan.

Funeral September, 1983

Two years later another procession
two brothers, three sisters carry him

this body harder to bear
we stumble under his weight.

A lone priest at the altar
chants the mass for the dead.

A storm rises, a wind gust
slams the church door
rattles windows.
His spirit restless, death
a mistake.

After the second funeral
my father stoops to place the velvet
ashes in the shade of two elms.
Releases a breath caught in his words
a benediction
a stifled farewell.

A handful of earth falls heavily
into the grave's precisely cut
mouth, a black hole
their ashes now side by side
imprisoned in boxes
inelegant homes.

Fifteen years later daffodils brush the black letters
cut into granite: *I have fought the good fight (Timothy 2)*

I dream my fingers into the earth
dream I disturb the grave, lift
their ashes and bone shards
into the wind at Birch Bay
a forest of silver bones, the wind
the only thief I trust.

Imagine

Two weeks before Chris dies
he explores the north:
rivers, mountains, moraines
slag heaps and wandering creeks
pans for gold at Bonanza Creek
gambles at Diamond Tooth Gertie's
paddles the Yukon river.
Visits the house where his dead
brother once lived.

Thirty years later I stand on the banks of that river
silenced by its width, its roar of rapids
imagine the thrill of deep currents pulling his canoe along
the midnight sun on his back.

Life drawing

When I draw my brother
from a photograph, the last
that was taken
a different face appears
my mother's twenty-year-old eyes
my sister's upturned lips.

These faces that keep appearing
are the variations of love
as I try to draw meaning
from his death at twenty-two.

I draw cheeks flushed against umber hair
his dripping paddle lifted
across the bow of his canoe

The graphite pencil breaks again
too brittle for his shy smile

Grief a jagged line
cuts into his face.

Travel

In the sanctuary, I light a candle
pray this single light will spiral
across the distance between
my son and me.

He's gone looking for his uncles
who never came back home.

He climbs to Everest's base camp, into a landscape
of myth: (young men die early in our family)
walks through India, Viet Nam, Cambodia.
Explores Thailand, Kaoshuing, the Phillipines, Bali –
retraces their steps in Yukon, the Arctic.

The stories of his uncles echo

I light another candle
a brave flicker in the lonely
December dark.

Granite

When my brothers crashed
we called them accidents
and chose to burn them
one at a time
bury their ashes under a slab
of grey granite.
We did not feed the earth
with their remains
denied them the final
maternal embrace.

Today I visit and touch
the cold marker: one stone
two brothers
an infant sister.
Trace the births, deaths
carved into my heart.

My father's ashes
lie near them
a few feet away —

He leans, I can feel him still
leaning into the impossible task
of keeping his children safe.

OTHERS

Rootbound

I and the ten thousand things are of one root

— Wan Shi

Something has come apart
pulled from shadows
into a tangled bog of memory
root bound.

Winter grips without break
paralyzing cold, the drag of my clothing
binds my limbs in damp feathers.

Grief's grimace: *the gnawing fang of melancholy*

Open and lift
the grey mask that covers
my eyes   my ears   my heart.

Give me birthing music, tell me how to breathe
open the heart
to spring's first leaves
their dazzling topaz.

Lead me to still waters
the endless blue sky
the kestrel's *ke-ree ke-ree*
mercy within mercy

Kyrie: spiritual surrender: cry of the soul changing.

I heard that once you buried someone you love
that piece of earth claims you
forever.

Soul

Is it breath that makes a soul?
Bodies formed around that pink ribbon of air —

> A premature nursery
> my hand reaches
> through the sterile porthole
> index finger strokes
> the bird-like chest
> a reminder
> to keep on breathing.

> This being
> size of a pound of butter —
> a living soul?

> What about the one
> in the corner left alone
> in the corner covered with a sheet
> sheltered from curious eyes

> the one lacking a forebrain: *prosencephalon absentia*
> brainstem intact — heart and lungs functioning
> the breath going in and out

> a sign: No Touch

> (touch prolongs life)

> breath ceased on the sixth day

Where did the soul go?

Sacrament

That April afternoon I washed her hair
smoothed it into the basin

poured warm water then poured again
rinsed warm water over her cool brow

Her son met me at the door, said
maybe we should wait.

I leaned towards her, whispered, I know
you love to have your hair washed.

Yes she murmured *Yes*
Her son crossed his arms and looked away —

Thank you thank you. Warm water spilled over
her brow, her neck and shoulders.

As I walked home I saw six white geese fly over
calling out their return home.

Migration

The Savannah sparrow on a bare branch
opens its beak and sings.
Its crisp *t-sip, t-sip,* not quite a vesper
for your friend's mother who died
a few days ago, but we pause, listen —
peer through bone branches
that await the soon-to-be-green.

The Savannah has returned on its spring migration to nest
in our fescue grasses. The yellow band above its eye
catches the light and it turns, looks at me, at you and
flits away. It knows nothing of your frustration with the weather
where snow drifts from the coulees across
the hills and onto the highway.

Spring is late. You curse the weather, a blizzard in May
heavy snowfall warning for the southwest, the spring
storm keeping you here beside me, instead of heading
down the highway to her funeral.

We walk the wide prairie morning and you tell me about
Lola, a war bride who kept her eight red-haired
children busy with chores while she smoked and read her
novels, feet propped up on a footstool. I think she
probably whistled while they worked.

The town beauty, she was always the one in fashion
shows: lean and tall with rich auburn hair, a lovely
Yorkshire accent. I never knew her but this morning you
showed me the Savannah sparrow and I will remember her now.

Beatrice

Why bend this beautiful light?
— John Livingstone Clark, *Body and Soul*

I don't want to be here, she tells me
tied to this bed, I can't get out.
My daughter put me here because she owes me money
wants to sell my house, keep the profits.
Do you think I'm crazy? I really shouldn't be here —
those nurses, they tie me down, and the food is awful.
What's that noise in the hallways? Is someone listening?

No doors
leading outside.

The Lord is my Shepherd, I shall not want. The clarity of her voice
down corridors as I walk toward her room, and from Timothy
about God giving us a spirit of courage, not cowardice
And Romans 5 — *we rejoice in our sufferings, knowing*
that suffering produces endurance, and endurance
produces character and character produces hope
and hope does not disappoint us.

Suffering, she scoffs, I know all about that, but I'm not alone
I've got the Lord Jesus Christ. Ask me my favourite book,
The Bible! as if it's a badge of sanity or grace
or a beacon of everlasting life.
A teacher's true authority, her words hover in the room
index finger stabbing the air, eyes looking towards heaven
She laughs at the absurdity of it all, says her friend
Alma will be in to take her home.

When I return a week later she's not there — they've taken her
a bowel resection at 87; the nurse tells me
she didn't tolerate surgery, is now in ICU

her mouth taped open
respirator rasps its in and out
inflating her lungs
forcing her heart to pump
lub dub lub dub

Her face, the strong features conformed around tubes
sharp edges dissolved, jaw gone slack, eyes half-open

Oh God.

Why ask God? it's the surgeon's knife that cut her light
gloved hands that sewed up that voice, stitched closed
the skin of her spirit.

Beatrice, I whisper, close to her ear. It's me. Stroke her forehead.
Looks like they finally shut you up.

She throws me a look of longing
of rage and helplessness, recognition and despair
disappointment
and character produces hope and hope does not disappoint us

But it does.

Her eyes close again, she shuts me out. Me, the tubes
the beeping monitors, nurses babbling "she's a little brighter
today."

I want to tell them about her voice, how it filled the room
with light, about her childhood in the north of England
her emigration to Montreal at the beginning of the century
her mother's garden, her estranged son on the coast
her absent daughter, friends she played cards with
her bright strong voice, her laugh, the light in her room
(did I say that?)
But she's gone.

Travelling back to that place behind her eyes
somewhere deep in a garden of light
a symphony playing Bach or Mozart
back to that place of beginning   a journey
to a cathedral of angels.

Two days later her heart
stops.   The line goes flat.

Why bend this beautiful light?

Sunday afternoon
For S. Padmanab

His poems speak the slow language
of love, his words a soft camera:
the morning's mangoes, smooth pears
plump strawberries, ruby pomegranate
yellow light on wooden chairs.

These words for his wife
and we bear witness — only
sit and sip tea.

He takes us to India, the crush of peacock
afternoons, savory heat: distant, exotic.
Introduces a shy bride, and *long-limbed men with pearly teeth*
about to board a train
lily ponds, bushes and ant mounds
now saffron, now indigo
now jacaranda green.

On this sad, windy afternoon
he tells us soon he too will board a train
travel toward an oasis of light.

Summer, 1995

My friend's daughter lies in a hospital bed
breathing but unresponsive.

A joy-ride on a long July night.
The end of a wild young summer.

Her words chip off like ice.

Tea goes cold on the table between us.

I walk home from the hospital
the moon silent above me.

Cars roar past, music
blaring, girls laughing

into the summer stillness.

Language fails

All grief, anyone's grief . . . is the weight of a sleeping child.
— Anne Michaels, *Fugitive Pieces*

At dinner she says
my friend's loss is unspeakable
. . . *unspeakable* she says.

Language fails
when we reach for words
to tell our story
words that stick in our throats
tongues heavy with grief
(the dead have stolen our tongues).

Mute with loss, confused,
we flail through days and nights.

Tears scorch our skin, burn our lips
as we try to pray.

We want our miserable prayers
to spiral unfathomable distance.

Points of light shrouded in grief.

My friend carries her sleeping child
comatose, months after the crash
asks her to wake up now —

She is comforted by Jakob's story,
an acknowledgement of loss,
as if tragedy places things
in a new order

all of us searching for that broken light.

Sweet old lady

You sit on the side of your bed rocking
a sad little tune dribbles between your lips
hair a froth of dream whip around your face
bright eyes falling back into your skull
that protrudes more each day.
I visit to test your blood sugar, talk about diabetes.

The first day I saw you I thought I had the wrong chart
thought I was in the wrong apartment
the stacked trays and boxes
marshmallow cookies frosted with toasted coconut
cream-filled bismarks baskets of donuts chocolate icing gone dry
cartons of COCA-COLA CLASSIC peppermints
and coloured gumdrops Lowney's Bridge Mix and Bassett's allsorts
McDonald's chocolate milkshake
butter tarts pecan pie macaroons.

Your family killing you with sweetness
your old feet gone black
flesh rotting your toes.

Rocking at the bedside
peeing into bedclothes
your legs too sore to stand on
the black creeping up
sweetness eating you alive.

Hard light
For Madeleine

Only God knows the words
for good-bye to a dying friend.
Beautiful this dying woman, her skin
an amber cloth on protruding bones.
Wing-like, her shoulders scaffold her shirt
yet her abdomen grows, liver spreading
around her middle, a flotation device
to carry her into the land of mandala
the portals open, in welcome.

This dying woman is beautiful
her spirit visible in November's waning light.
I bless her with water, with words.
A final embrace. Moments of the holy
I carry with me.

When I return home the cold descends sharply
days darken into winter, wind howls its fierce warning.
A few days on John calls
"she collapsed, her legs gave way
she could not get up."
He pulled her along the floor
back to bed cradling her
with kindness
and worn out arms.

Tears drip off my cheeks
I drive the bleak and lonely streets
of Saskatchewan winter.

Voices

Grandpa hears voices in his head
while he rounds up horses with his uncle Ike.
Harry Mason corners them, pens them.
Grandpa talks to his prize Percheron
smoothes her glossy mane, coal black.

He smiles past us, all who stand at his bedside.

He's out on the land dying
in front of us, calling, calling
to all the pretty horses
who run in verdant fields.

He coaxes them, his voice calm, loving
reaches out and strokes the bedclothes
alive in his grasp.

Grandma Rose hears voices outside her head:
they tell her it's time to get up, eat
go to bed, hands on her thinning body
bones thrust between cold sheets
rough hands turn and position her.
That old anger, his hands on her, rough and quick.
She turns away, weeps into the bedclothes.

Her eyes search the room
for kindness. She waits
for the mercy
of morning.

She has lost her voice
unable to call out, even for water.
She reaches out to me, a frightened
unbroken horse, to free her
from this prison of tight white sheets.

Waiting

In a cold room down the street
my grandmother's dying alone.

Upstairs the children sleep next to me.
The party goes ahead as planned
downstairs music blaring.
I cannot feel my feet
numb from so much standing
waiting by her bedside.

Waiting for my first child,
Grandmother taught me
to sow a garden, till the earth
drop seeds into furrows
wait for the spring of green.

My own mother, busy with children
had no time to garden
no time to tend green shoots
that showed themselves each year
no time to weed out noxious infiltrators.
She went to bed with a migraine.
arm over her eyes to keep out light, noise
the sight of us.

Grandma came then
told jokes, we laughed
quietly. She planted seeds in the garden
sent us to pull weeds, waiting
out mother's headache.

I hated the garden then. The unforgiving sun
pushed me down into the hard clay, no shade.
Dirt held nasty weeds, a grip so tight
we needed a knife to cut them out.

Dream

I dream Pablo Neruda gives me a ladder
tells me to pull myself up
straps tucked along the sides

I try to climb out
grab one rung at a time
cannot lift one foot
onto the next rung
I slide down
fall on my knees

My pockets are empty
My hands are bleeding

Spade

I learn the heart
is the same size as a fist
its shape like a spade.

My heart's edges
have dulled with digging
my love tamped down
under the weight of grief.

Faith lies in a fallow field
a garden
long since harvested.

My fist opens
over my heart.

Ghosts

Is it wind that brings the ghosts
hurrying them into corners
lurking in the cobwebs of memory
or hiding behind doors, like Boo Radley?

Is it winter when they return? The cold blue northern
blasting them into our dreams, rattling windows
whistling their disapproval, demanding to be heard.

Or do ghosts like summer best? Sailing in on a warm breeze
a still summer night, hovering above gardens, tinkling wind
chimes. The hostas waltzing, ferns ruffling, leaves whispering.

Do they arrive in spring when March winds
shake the sleeping branches? Snow falls to the ground
a heavy cloak, shed all at once.
Ghosts shouting injunctions to tree roots: wake up
pay attention!

They walk among us in all seasons
do their bidding when they please —
A flash of memory, a song, a sidelong look.
A dream, a pause, a phrase.

A wind gust from somewhere, blowing.

Every word I have spoken the wind has taken, as it will take me.

— Michael Crummey, *Her Mark*